OTHER BOOKS BY LESLIE LEE

*Backcountry Ranger
in Glacier National Park, 1910-1913:
The Diaries and Photographs
of Norton Pearl*
Published 1994

* * *

Sacred Space: Pine Hollow
Published 2014

* * *

We Are the Land: Ireland
Published 2019

LeeStudioTC.com

Contents

	List of Illustrations, Maps, and Charts	v
	Your Itinerary	vi
	Your Calendar	vii
	Preface	xii
I.	Early People, DNA, and the Ice Age	1
II.	Archeology and the Megalithic Culture	5
III.	Invasions, Mythology, and the Celts	9
IV.	The Land of Saints and Scholars, Vikings, Normans, Scots-Irish, and the English	11
V.	Regions to Explore:	19
	Southwest Ireland	21
	Northwest Ireland	29
	Northeast Ireland	35
	Southeast Ireland	41
VI.	Irish Mythology	49
VII.	Chief Irish Festivals and Gods	59
VIII.	Ancient Irish Law	61
IX.	Trees	63

Appendices

Appendix 1. Pronunciation of Modern Irish 66
Appendix 2. Irish Place Names 68
Appendix 3. Your Family Tree 70
Appendix 4. Travel List of Items to Pack for Ireland 71
Appendix 5. Travel Tips for Packing for Ireland 73
Appendix 6. Irish Timeline 77
Appendix 7. Prehistoric Timeline 90

BOOK 2 *Leslie's* **TRAVEL COMPANION**

Leslie's Field Guide to *Ireland*

WRITTEN AND ILLUSTRATED BY LESLIE LEE

LESLIE LEE PUBLISHER
TRAVERSE CITY, MICHIGAN

Ways to Use This Book

This pocket-sized field guide can hold your itineraries, calendars, data, notes, maps, and charts. Its small size makes it ideal to carry everywhere on your trip. Along the way, jot down notes of favorite places and people and add quick sketches in the margins and on the blank pages. When you return, this little book will be a cherished memento of the trip itself and a handy reminder for return trips.

Text and Illustrations © 2020 Leslie Lee

ALL RIGHTS RESERVED. No part of this publication may be reproduced, stored in a retrieval system, or transmitted in any form or by any means electronic, mechanical, photocopying, recording or otherwise, without the prior written permission of the publisher.

Leslie Lee Publisher
Traverse City, Michigan
LeeStudioTC.com

ISBN: 978-0-9915022-9-5

Illustrations: Leslie Lee
Editor: Jennifer Carroll
Interior design and layout: Yvonne Fetig Roehler
Project coordination by Jenkins Group, Inc.
www.BookPublishing.com

Printed in the United States of America
24 23 22 21 20 • 5 4 3 2 1

List of Illustrations, Maps, and Charts

Driving Map of Ireland viii
Driving Tips and Times ix
Provinces of Ireland x
Ancient Roads of Ireland xi
The Barn at the Flax Cottage xiii
The Steppes Grassland and Ice Age Refuges xiv
The Natural Rock Stack at the Cliffs of Moher 3
Tomb Types and Megaliths 4
DNA Lines of Ireland Chart 6
Ancient Territories of Ireland 8
Carrowmore's Oldest Dolmen in County Sligo 10
Garfinny Bridge 15
Walking on Slievemore, Achill Island 18
Glandore Harbor, County Cork 19
Southwest Region of Ireland Map 23
Southwest Cork and the Blackwater River Valley Map 27
Northwest Region of Ireland Map 31
Achill Island, Keem Beach 33
Northeast Region of Ireland Map 37
Southeast Region of Ireland Map 43
Boyne River Valley Map 44
Fireplace at Bushmills 58
Entrance at Six-Thousand-Year-Old Megalith at Knowth 60
Illustration of Ogham Stones 62
The Brian Boru Oak 64
The Ogham Alphabet 65
Musicians at O'Connor's Pub in Doolin 76
Entrance at Six-Thousand-Year-Old Newgrange 89
Prehistoric Timeline 90
Counties of Ireland .... Back Cover

Itinerary

Calendar

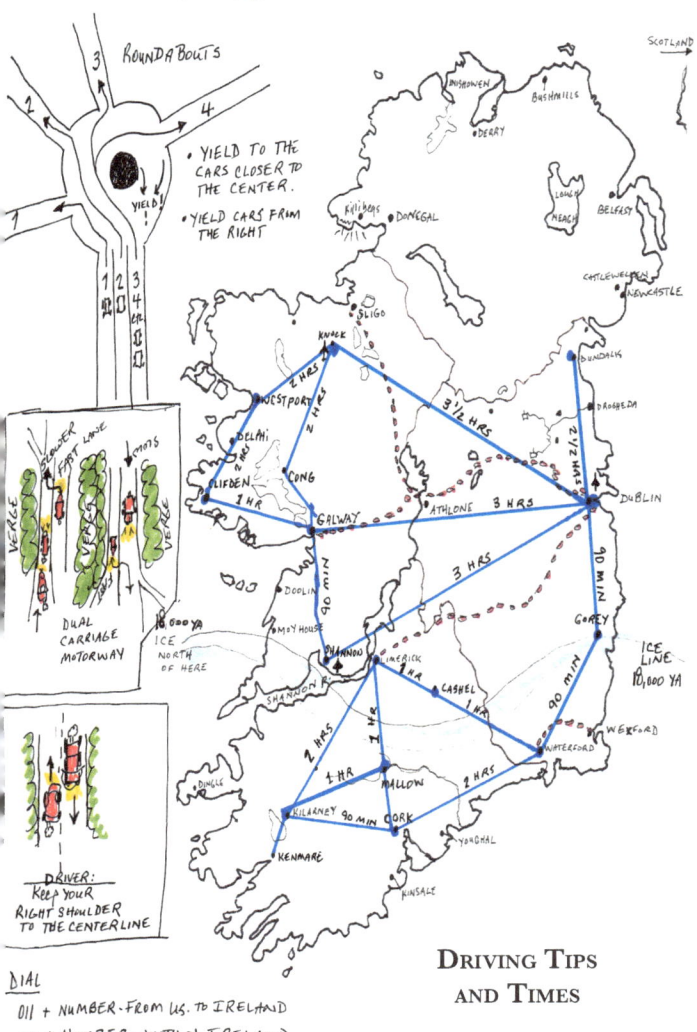

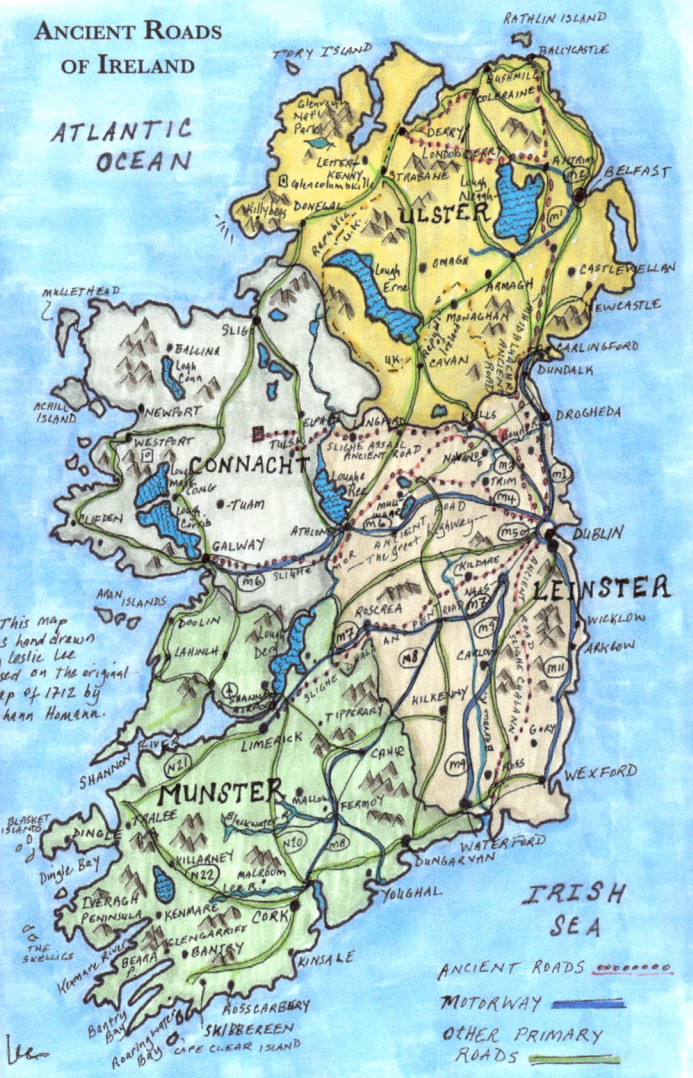

Preface

I'm not a geneticist, a historian, or a teacher. I wasn't born or raised in Ireland though my direct maternal ancestry is Irish. I am, however, a student of many and varied subjects and I'm intensely interested in the deep history of my ancestral people.

This book is much like the handmade field guide I prepared for my family and friends before our trip to Ireland to search for our ancestors and learn about the land and people of Ireland in person. In order to better appreciate my short time there, I studied before we left. I then wrote up my notes, and drew the maps based on an original antique map in 1712 by Johann Baptist Homann, and illustrated the charts for a pocket-sized spiral-bound hand-written study guide for each of us. These contained our itineraries, data, maps, and charts that we could carry everywhere. Along the way, we jotted down our notes of favorite places and people, adding quick sketches. With the itinerary and calendar pasted in the front, the little book became a cherished memento of the trip itself and a handy reminder for return trips.

Whatever small amount I learned vastly improved my experience in Ireland. I'm still learning. I apologize for any mistakes—they're all mine. I've done my best to include correct dates for prehistoric events, but rather than use the words "approximately, about, sort of, some of," I've taken the liberty to simply state the date I thought was best. I welcome referenced corrections through my website LeeStudioTC.com.

To all the Irish I've met on my visits who are of the land, who have opened their doors, their hearts, and shared their spirit with me, "Go raibh maith agut." Thank you.

The barn at the Flax Cottage.

THE STEPPES GRASSLAND AND ICE AGE REFUGES

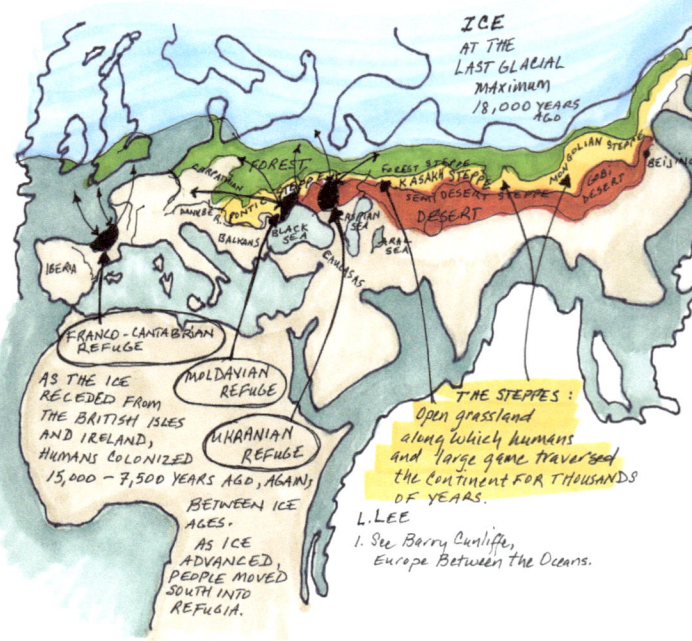

I

Early People, DNA, and the Ice Age

The Steppes Grassland and Ice Age Refuges

What was the land like at the dawn of modern humans? Imagine a blank sheet of ice covering the northern hemisphere to around the fiftieth parallel, not far from modern Moscow. A polar desert covered the area south of it for hundreds of miles. South of that stretched a giant swath of tundra, or grassy steppe, from east to west from Mongolia to the Balkans like a conveyor belt for large game and the humans who hunted them.

Three times in fifty thousand years advancing glaciers forced entire populations into pockets of refuge before warming climates melted receding glaciers into lakes and rivers, once again creating the life-giving steppes. During these times of warmth, people moved north into Britain,

Ireland, Norway, and along the northern coastlines. Masses of people grouped up, hunted, interbred, and retreated to refuges when the glaciers returned. They continued to interbreed and migrate in complicated patterns of meeting and separating. One can visualize not a family tree, but a great river delta of crisscrossing ancestries.

These were the hunter-gatherers of the Mesolithic Era and they formed the bedrock genes in Eurasia and Western Europe referred to as Basal Eurasians.

The ice age of twenty thousand years ago created so much polar ice that ocean levels dropped four hundred feet. Any artifacts of earlier ice ages would be under the water of that now submerged coastline. When it was cold and dry, the English Channel and the Celtic Sea were frozen land across which humans and game traveled on one side or the other of the single Rhine-Thames River. Genetic echoes of this division are seen in inhabitants of East Coast England differing from those who arrived in West England, West Scotland, and Ireland on the southwest side of the great river.

In times of glacial advance, the most western of these hunter-gatherers took refuge in the Basque territory on the northern border of what are now Spain and France. Experts call it the Franco-Cantabrian refuge.

Archeological evidence places people in Ireland nine thousand years ago. Artifacts from earlier inhabitants are off the coast, submerged under the ocean from a time when glaciers took up that much more water before again melting.

Eight thousand years ago, farmers from the Near East began to move west along the Mediterranean Sea reaching Western Europe, Sardinia, and the Isles. Within a thousand years the male farming genes of G mixed with those of the early hunter-gatherers. Female DNA lines of J and K traveled with them.

The natural rock stack at the Cliffs of Moher.

II

ARCHEOLOGY AND THE MEGALITHIC CULTURE

MEGALITHS

Who built the great so-called Irish *passage tombs* of Newgrange, Knowth, Dowth, and Loughcrew? They seem to me to be ceremonial centers rather than tombs. These older-than-the-pyramids constructions were gigantic mounds of dry laid stone. Inside, chambers were laid out for the ceremonies and rituals of the druids to ensure bountiful harvests and fertility. Were the builders of these structures early farmers who then mixed with Mesolithic Era hunter-gatherers as they moved north into Ireland? Sardinian women of the H3 line traveled with the hunter-gatherers of the G2 farming and I hunter-gatherer Y DNA lines. Perhaps it was these people who formed the core of the Atlantic Megalithic Culture and built the great stone structures.

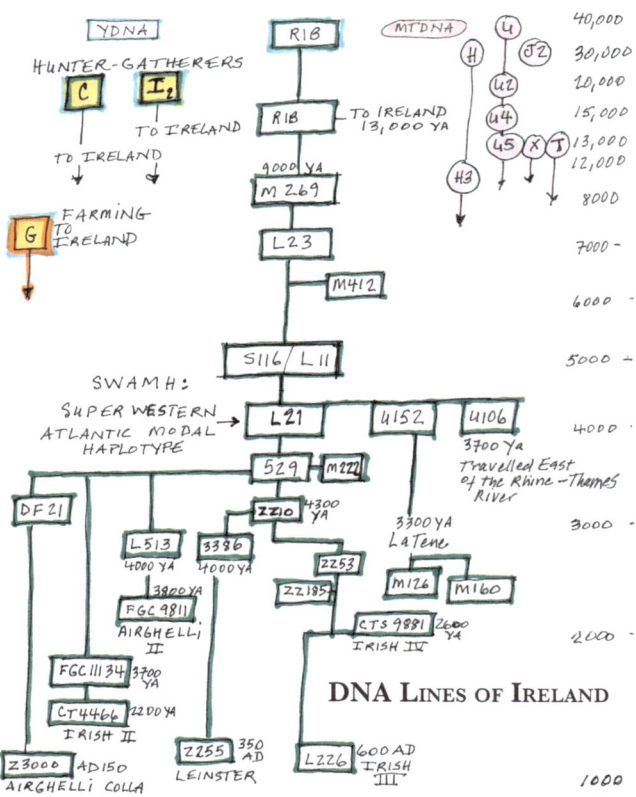

Y DNA

To understand the Celts, or Gaels, it is important to understand a little about male DNA. Geneticists examine the Y chromosome of men to measure the distance between mutations to determine the passage of time. Like a clock, it measures time and marks it with a mutation. Y is the male line sex chromosome. Men also carry the X chromosome of the maternal line, or mitochondrial line often referred to as MT DNA, however, men cannot pass down MT DNA to their offspring. Only women pass mitochondrial DNA to their children. The mutations themselves are like a roadmap of ancestry.

The most successful male line in the British Isles and Ireland was called R1B1. It was called the Atlantic Modal Haplotype, or L-23 as well. As with H on the female side, R1B1 came to dominate the genetic pool. Clan mother H, or Helena, remained one of the bedrock maternal genetic lines. Maternal DNA lines tend to be stable, ancient, and regional. The AMH-R1B1 men of five thousand years ago wiped out nearly all of the extant hunter-gatherer, Basal European, and farming genes of the men before them. Most of the G2 and I men were no more. This is possible with male genes simply because men can procreate many times over with many women over the course of a long life. Women cannot because of the time needed to carry a baby to term. So if male lines dominate a culture, they will also dominate the genes of the male offspring.

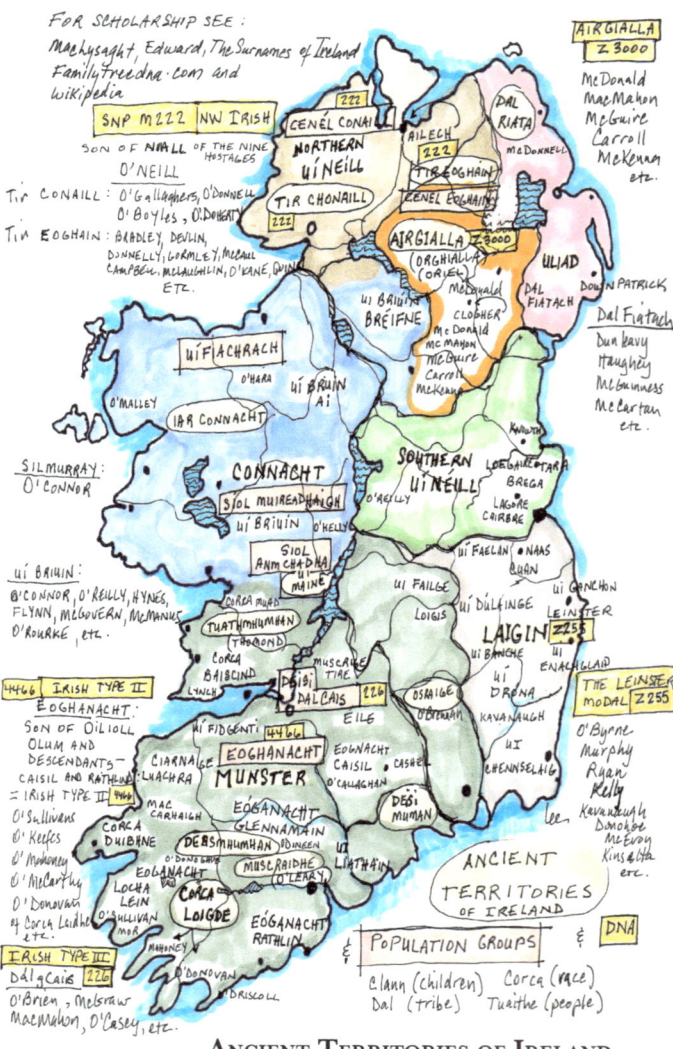

III

INVASION, MYTHOLOGY, AND THE CELTS

THE GREAT FLOOD AND THE CELTS

The seas rose creating the British Isles and Ireland as separate from the continent for the last time around seven thousand five hundred years ago. Rising sea levels broke through the Bosporus into the Black Sea creating the epic flood of Noah and Gilgamesh. The flow of saltwater pouring into the freshwater lake was two hundred times the amount of water that flows over Niagara Falls every day. This caused the level of the lake-sea to rise six inches a day without pause.

All of the people living on the banks of the now salty Black Sea needed to move away from the shorelines. Seeking freshwater once again, life needed to move away or up the Rivers Dnieper, Dniester, and the Danube away from the flooding shoreline in a great diaspora.

This is what happened with the R1B1 men from the Pontic steppes. The word *Pontic* refers to the region around the Black Sea. They were early Bronze Age warrior-traders of five thousand years ago from the Pontic Steppe north of the Black Sea that geneticists have since identified. These nomadic herders of cattle domesticated the horse, perfected the wheel and cart, and formed an aristocratic warrior society. They were on the move west until they could travel west no further—to Ireland five thousand years ago. They brought horses, metalworking, and the Indo-European language. They brought their genes—Celtic genes.

Geneticist David Reich tells us in *Who We Are and How We Got Here* that the DNA of Irish men is ten percent first farmers and a whopping ninety percent Bell Beaker people of the Pontic Steppes. When they arrived five thousand years ago they soon dominated the existing communal, female-worshipping, megalith-building, place-based early farming communities of Ireland.

Carrowmore's oldest dolmen in County Sligo.

IV

THE LAND OF SAINTS AND SCHOLARS, VIKINGS, NORMANS, SCOTS-IRISH, AND THE ENGLISH

CHRISTIANITY

While Ireland was never invaded by Rome, nor part of the Roman Empire, missionary Christians traveled to and from Europe spreading the religion. Saint Patrick, the most famous of these, was not, however the earliest. The Irish adopted early Christian practices in the fifth century establishing monasteries for worship, scholarship, and community across Ireland throughout the sixth and seventh centuries. These served as sanctuaries of learning for scholars and theologians in Ireland and from across the world, and were revered for their collections of illuminated manuscripts and development of libraries. During the Dark Ages and Early Medieval Period in Europe, Ireland became known as *The Land of Saints and Scholars*.

VIKINGS

Raiding Vikings in the 800s and 900s ransacked monasteries. First, the Norse arrived, followed by the Danes. They stole treasures, burned monasteries, and fought each other and the Irish. Vikings developed the first towns such as Dublin, Cork, Wexford, Waterford and Limerick. Some intermarried with the native Irish and settled in. For two centuries Ireland suffered further depredations until the Vikings lost to the warriors of Brian Boru, high king of Ireland, at the Battle of Clontarf in 1014 in which Brian Boru was killed. As a secondary power, some Vikings remained.

NORMANS, ENGLISH, AND SCOTS-IRISH

From the 1100s to the 1600s, Ireland was dominated by Normans from England and Wales who imposed an English feudal-merchant system on the prior Irish system of provincial and territorial kings and high kings. Over time, their population blended with many of the native Irish. When England sent over Protestant English and Scots in the 1600s to subdue and dominate the native Irish Catholics, the Normans in Ireland became known as *Old English*. Depending on their circumstances, intermarriages, and alliances, they either fared well or poorly when the Protestants arrived to take over. While the Old English Normans and the Protestant English and Scots carved out territory and property for their own people in this fertile, productive land, the native Irish endured their domination and struggled to survive.

Many Americans proudly claim *Scotch-Irish* heritage, but some may be a bit foggy about who they were. They were not Scots and Irish who had intermarried as some of us imagined. No, the Scots-Irish and the native Irish were enemies. The Scots were Protestants who had been granted Irish land in the 1600s in the Province of Ulster by the British in order to colonize and subdue the Catholic natives. In Ireland, the Scots-Irish call themselves *Ulster-Scots*. By the middle of the 1600s, one hundred thousand Scots lived in Ireland mainly working in retting, weaving, and milling linen. The English Protestants who arrived at this time were called Settlers, or Planters, and the lands they confiscated were called plantations.

Unlike the Norman-English, when these new English arrived, they carried out a thorough colonization designed to subjugate and destroy the local inhabitants. They began quietly as their surveyors reshaped districts, parishes, and dioceses, and renamed towns and provinces. They imposed the English language and followed by filling positions of authority with their own. They then forcibly confiscated the land for a relatively tiny ruling elite who wielded enormous power. Forests were cut to build ships and longbows.

In the Tudor Period between 1485 and 1603, the Church of England was created as a combination of Catholic and Protestant practices designed to unify England. But this new church of Anglicans with its Catholic ways rankled many Protestant Ulster-Scots and English Planters in Ireland who refused to adopt it. For this, they were removed from government, civil, and military positions of power. These English economic sanctions, religious persecutions, and replacements by Anglicans in the 1700s prompted the Ulster-Scots to look toward America. Many emigrated once again. The deep resentment felt by these dispossessed Ulster-Scots for the fickle Anglican English later fueled the armies of the American Revolution to victory against the British.

CROMWELL'S CONQUEST OF IRELAND

In 1628, Oliver Cromwell came to power. Revered in England and reviled in Ireland, he and his troops laid siege to Irish cities between 1649 and 1653. They butchered inhabitants and confiscated their land. Moving through the countryside they massacred so many native Irish, only a third of the former population remained when they were done. With notable cruelty, Cromwell forbade Catholic worship and imposed penal laws on the remaining locals. Even after his death, the English confiscation of Ireland continued.

They seized an additional eleven million acres of land for their own, closed schools, and banished the remaining Irish Catholics of the region to live west of the Shannon River on the poorest land. The Catholics in Ulster fared a similar fate. By 1703, only fourteen percent of Irish land was owned by the native Irish.

The Irish fought for their land, their people, and their beliefs, holding on as best they could, even as the next hundred years saw unrelieved devastation for them. Laws against Catholics and the Irish woolen trade were enacted. Battles raged. While England turned its armies and fleets to put down the rebellion in the American colonies, the Irish pushed for reforms only to again suffer English domination through the remainder of the century.

Garfinny Bridge on the Dingle Peninsula across which the English marched their troops.

THE GREAT FAMINE

During the Great Famine, potato blight repeatedly wiped out the major food source for the Irish from 1845 through 1849. Ireland was ruled by Britain. Many English landowners in Ireland exacerbated Irish misery by forcibly evicting Irish tenants from their estates. Homeless, the native Irish of all ages suffered the elements of nature, disease, and death. By 1853, a quarter of a million Irish were permanently expelled from their small crofts on English-Irish estates. The ruthlessness of these clearances to rid English estates in Ireland of poor smallholders left a legacy of enduring hatred for the landed gentry of England, the richest country in the world. Some experts claim the English in Ireland continued to eat a varied diet, and moreover, exported Irish wheat, butter, beef, and lamb to England and their distant colonies during the famine. Two million native Irish people—of a population of eight million—starved, died of disease, or emigrated by 1859.

THE TROUBLES AND GOVERNING IRELAND

It's difficult for an outsider to understand the conflicts between Northern Ireland and the Republic of Ireland, however, some mention must be made so visitors will have some sensitivity to it. The primary conflict within Northern Ireland has been between native Irish Catholics and Protestant English and Scots who immigrated there when England colonized much of the Province of Ulster. The issues centered on the native Irish having been forced to give up their land and independence. In addition, many in the Republic of Ireland wished for a unified Ireland. The long-term, often impassioned, sometimes violent warring is referred to as *The Troubles*.

There is a border between the Republic of Ireland and Northern Ireland that most people are thankful is only on a map.

The Republic of Ireland is part of the European Union (EU) whose currency is the euro. The Republic of Ireland does not have a queen, or any royalty. The IRA refers to the Irish Republican Army. Sinn Fein is a political party. Representatives of the *Dáil Éireann*, the legislature, govern the Republic of Ireland.

Six counties of Northern Ireland are part of the United Kingdom and the EU (for the moment). Their currency is the pound sterling. The United Kingdom of Northern Ireland has the same queen and royalty of England. The Ulster-Scots and English Planter people of the six counties that make up Northern Ireland of the United Kingdom of Britain are historically termed Loyalists.

Both the Republic of Ireland and Northern Ireland have a complicated, divisive history not dealt with here. The Good Friday Agreement of 1998 redistributed power between Northern Ireland and the Republic of Ireland. Even though the future is ambiguous, most people everywhere in Ireland want peace.

Walking on Slievemore past the abandoned village on Achill Island.

V

REGIONS TO EXPLORE

The following maps are hand-drawn based on an antique atlas and are not to scale. I've added a few places of interest to me to provide a quick way for the reader and traveling companions to choose where to visit. Of course, there are many more interesting places to visit than I was able to put on the map, so do explore. Always use an up-to-date driving map. I prefer a folded Michelin map of Ireland and the spiral-bound Collins road atlas.

Glandore Harbor in County Cork.

Southwest Ireland

Mostly in the Province of Munster

Southwest Region
Places of Interest

- Connemara, for scenic beauty north of Galway
- Surfing in Fanore on the west coast south of Galway
- Thoor Ballylee Tower House southeast of Galway
- Clonmacnoise, early intact monastic site and castle south of Athlone
- Meehambee megalith south of Athlone

- Clare Heritage Center south of the Burren
- The Burren, and Burren National Park, south of Galway in the Province of Connacht
- The Burren Perfumery, south of Galway
- Poulnabrone portal tomb/dolmen in the Burren south of Galway
- Gleninsheen megalithic tomb in the Burren
- Ailwee Caves near Ballyvaughn north in the Burren
- Ballykinvarga (Kilfenora)-Iron Age stone fort near the Burren
- Dysert O'Dea Monastery/Archeology Center south of the Burren
- Corcomroe Abbey north of the Burren

- Cragganowen Center north of Limerick
- Hunt museum in Limerick
- St. John's Castle in Limerick

- Carrigaforte west of Limerick
- Cashel (Eoganacht) 9000 years ago in the east of the Province of Munster
- Knockcurraghbola wedge tomb in County Tipperary
- In Tipperary, horses, hunting and hurling
- Lough Gur Mesolithic Interpretive Center south of Limerick
- Adare Village south of Limerick
- Holy Isle off Killaloe in Lough Derg north of Limerick

- Traditional music in Doolin (and anywhere) on the west coast
- In Corofin town, the Clare Heritage and Genealogical Center
- Aran Islands/The Black Fort on the island of Inish Mor off of Doolin
- Cliffs of Moher on the west coast near Doolin
- Inchiquin Castle of the O'Briens east of Doolin
- Leamaneh Castle "Red Mary" east of Doolin
- Coole Park near Gort east of Doolin
- Dun Aonghasa on the the Aran Island of Inish Mor
- Dun Conor on the Aran Island of Inish Mean

- Ratoo round tower north of Tralee
- Kerry Woolen Mills in Beaufort west of Killarney
- On Lough Leane in County Kerry, Innisfallen/Ross Island near Killarney

- Ring of Kerry, on the Iveragh Peninsula in the southwest
- Killarney National Park at the base of the Iveragh Peninsula
- Skellig Michael off the Iveragh Peninsula
- Staige stone fort on the Iveragh Peninsula
- Beehive Huts and many archeological sites on the Dingle Peninsula (take the tour)
- Dunbeg Fort near the end of the Dingle Peninsula
- Boat ride to the Blasket Islands from Dingle on the Dingle Peninsula
- Allihies Mining Museum on the Beara Peninsula
- Fastnet Lighthouse off the Mizen Head Peninsula, tour leaves from Baltimore
- Mizen Head museum on the end of the Mizen Head Peninsula

- Blarney Castle and grounds near Cork City
- In Cork/Cobh, the museum of the famine and immigration
- Kinsale, sailing and fine dining on the south coast
- Fota House Arboretum near Cork
- Skibbereen Heritage Center on the south coast
- Drombeg Stone Circle near Glandore on the south coast
- Whale watching from Baltimore on the south coast

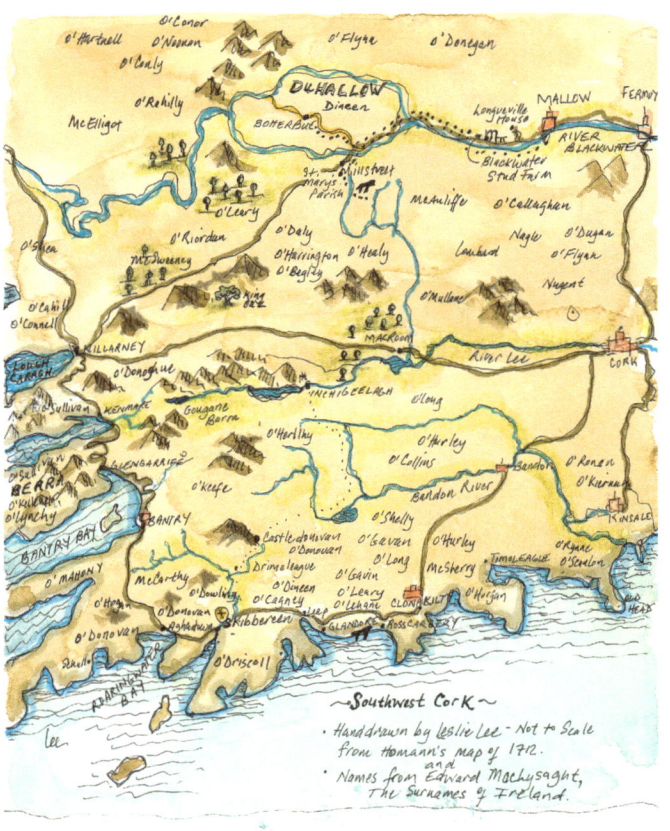

SOUTHWEST CORK
AND THE BLACKWATER RIVER VALLEY

Northwest Ireland

Mostly in the Province of Connacht

NORTHWEST IRELAND

SLIGHE ASSAIL ANCIENT ROADWAY
• • • • • • •   BEFORE AD 123
                 to Tara.

—•—•—•— Border of Republic of Ireland
         and Northern Ireland U.K.

NORTHWEST REGION
OF IRELAND

MULLET PENINSULA
Ceide Fields
MAYO
NEPHIN BEG MTS.
BALLINA
LOUGH CONN
Ballycroy Nat'l Park
ACHILL I.
OX MTS.
FOXFORD
museum
NEWPORT
Round Tower
Clew Bay
Srahwee
WESTPORT
CROAGH PATRICK
Partry Mts.
Doo Lough
Delphi
Abbey
Visitor Cen
Lough Carra
LOUGH MASK
kilma
CONG
SKY Road
Clifden
LOUGH CORRIB

Slieve League

High and Ro...

Northwest Region
Places of Interest

- Glenveagh National Park, County Donegal
- Flight of the Earls Heritage Center north of Derry/Londonderry on the north coast
- Kilclooney Dolmen north of Donegal near the west coast
- Glencolumbkille northwest of Donegal on the west coast
- Museum of Country Life in County Mayo
- Ballintubber Abbey north of Cong in County Mayo

* * *

- Cliffs of Magho, northeast of Sligo
- Carrowmore-Knocknarea south of Sligo, Queen Maeve's tomb (the Earth goddess and legendary queen of Connacht who sent armies against Cuculainn)
- Creevykeel court cairn north of Sligo on the west coast
- Carrowkeel megalithic center south of Sligo and west of Lough Arrow
- Enniskillen Islands in Lough Erne east of Sligo
- Carrowmore dolmen, stone circle, and megalithic center south of Sligo
- Crough Patrick mountain south of Westport
- Srahwee dolmen southwest of Westport
- Sky road at Roseleague Manor, north of Clifden in County Galway

- Delphi Lodge, Leenane, for fishing north of Clifden, south of Westport
- Achill Island for writers and artists, west from Newport on the west coast
- Rath Croghan from 9000 years ago, near Tulsk/Cruachain Ai Visitor Center, north of Lough Ree in County Roscommon, west of Longford, near the middle of Ireland
- Ceide Fields settlement from 9000 years ago on the north coast of County Mayo west of Sligo
- Dolmen west of Ceide Fields
- Castle Coole, south end of Lough Erne
- Museum of Country Life in County Mayo east of Westport

Keem Beach on Achill Island.

Northeast Ireland

Mostly in the Province of Ulster

NORTHEAST IRELAND

SLIGHE MIDLUACHRA
Ancient road before AD123.–To Tara.

Northeast Region of Ireland

Places of Interest

- Downhill strand in County Derry for surfing and parasailing northeast of Derry/Londonderry
- Mountains of Mourne for hiking south of Newcastle
- Beltany stone circle south of Derry/Londonderry
- Grianan of Aileach, ringfort of the Ui Neill north of Derry/Londonderry
- Famine Village on the north coast of the Inish Owen Peninsula
- Dunseverick castle on the north coast near Rathlin Island
- Lough-na-Crannagh on the northeast coast south of Rathlin Island
- Ossian's grave north of Glenariff on the northeast coast
- The Ulster Way—fourteen walks in the northeast
- Glenariff is beautiful—with a forest park in the northeast
- Giant's Causeway on the north coast
- Mount Sandel in County Derry, a Mesolithic Era settlement near Coleraine in the north

- Knockmany megalith northwest of Armagh
- Ulster-American Folk Park north of Omagh
- Beaghmore megalith west of Lough Neagh
- Ulster Folk and Transport Museum in Belfast

- Navan Fort (Emain Macha), the royal site of the kings of Ulster west of Armagh
- Haughey's Fort two miles from Navan Fort had high banks, deep ditches, pools, and large dogs
- Mount Stewart near the Strangford Lough on the east coast
- Davagh Forest Park west of Lough Neagh

- Castleward megalith south of Stranford Lough
- Castlewellan Forest Park north of Newcastle
- Southwest of Down Patrick, a megalith
- Ballynoe stone circle near Castlewellan
- Legananny dolmen north of Castlewellan
- Carrickfergus Castle on the east coast north of Lough Larne
- Castle Coole near Enniskillen south end of Lough Erne

- Proleek dolmen west of Carlingford
- The Tain Way, County Armagh—a walk through the Cooley Peninsula
- Slieve Gullion Forest Park north of Dundalk

Southeast Ireland

Mostly in the Province of Leinster

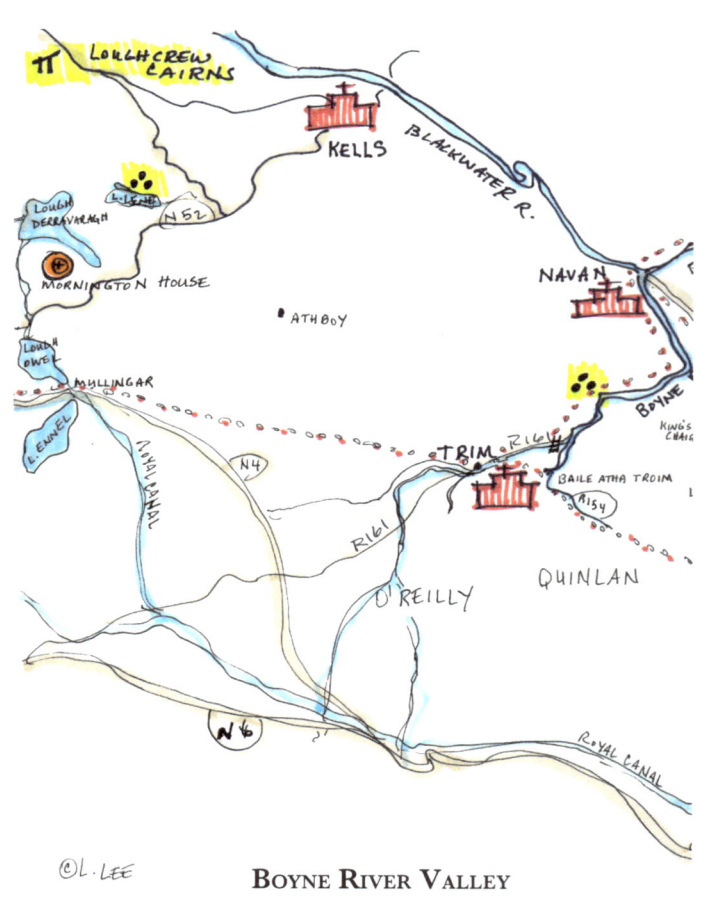

Boyne River Valley

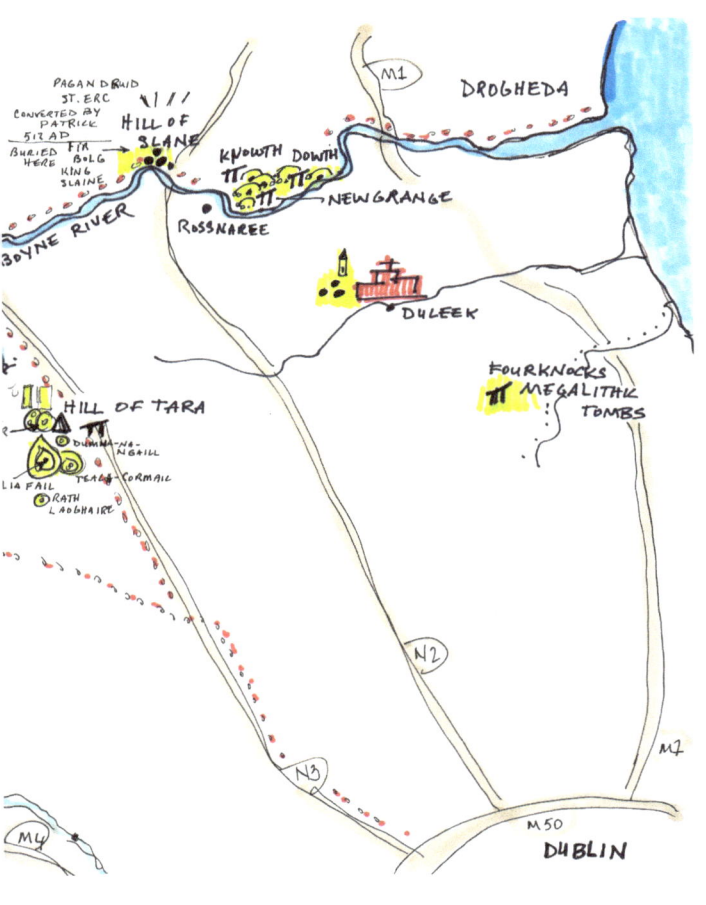

Southeast Region
Places of Interest

Boyne River Valley West of Drogheda

- Newgrange megalithic ceremonial center
- Knowth and Dowth megalithic ceremonial centers
- Hill of Tara, royal seat of ancient kings and queens, south of Navan
- Loughcrew megaliths and the Hill of the Witches northwest of Kells: thirty passage tombs over three hilltops where the Hay and Fairy Queen was mistress to all Ireland
- Uisneach hill, traditional center of Ireland west of Mullingar, hill of the bonfires
- Dun Ailinne—royal center of the kings of Leinster southeast of Kildare
- Fourknocks megalith south of Drogheda east of the Hill of Tara

* * *

- Clonmacnoise, early monastic site south of Athlone
- Castle at Rosecrea south of Tullamore, north of Cashel, east of Nenagh
- Durrow high cross north of Tullamore, west of Dublin
- Charleville castle south of Tullamore
- Tullamore Heritage Center at Tullamore
- Kildare village west and south of Dublin
- Naas horse racing southwest of Dublin

In and around Dublin

- Book of Kells at Trinity College
- The National Library
- National Museum of Ireland
- National Gallery
- Genealogical Office on Kildare Street
- Dublin Castle
- St. Patrick's Cathedral
- Ardgillan Castle north of Dublin
- Christ Church Cathedral
- Malahide Castle
- Glasnevin Cemetery Museum
- And so much more

* * *

- Waterford Castle, a well-kept secret just east of Waterford City
- Views from the Knockmealdown mountains north of Dungarvin on the south coast
- Swallows in the round tower of Ardmore northeast of Youghal on the south coast
- Famine ship near New Ross north of Waterford
- Rock of Cashel, folk village, and the Brian Boru center near Cashel north of Youghal

* * *

- Glendalough monastic site west of Wicklow
- Dunlavin dolmen west of Wicklow, south of Naas
- Castleruddery stone circle south of Naas and west of Wicklow

- Kilkenny craft village near Kilkenny north of Waterford
- Brownshill dolmen northeast of Carlow, northeast of Kilkenny, west of Wicklow
- Wicklow mountains and National Park south of Dublin, northwest of Wicklow
- Avoca weavers in Avoca village, south of Wicklow

VI

IRISH MYTHOLOGY

Interestingly, though written history doesn't always match with modern knowledge, mythology often does. I was surprised to discover that important climatic events were regularly represented in Irish mythology.

We European-Americans don't have much mythology to anchor ourselves to the past, unlike people of the old world who are raised with these stories from the time they are children. The legend of Paul Bunyan was scarcely two hundred years ago. Our mythology isn't older than this. Native American mythology is rich and varied, but we newcomers aren't usually taught that. Learning the rudiments of the stories of Ireland that stretched far before modern history was yet another fundamental aspect of traveling to Ireland to enrich my stay. Irish mythology reflects geological advances, retreats, and floods, and the invasions of people surprisingly well. Invasion, to me, means military conquering of established inhabitants. But in the context of the mythology, an invasion may just as easily mean a migrating population.

The Book of Invasions, an oral history, also known as *Lebor Gabala Erenn*, records the six sets of peoples and events that took place from the beginning of time in Ireland to the Middle Ages. Oral history was a form of passing knowledge from one generation to the next without losing the power of the information, something like trade secrets of today. The recipients of this knowledge were called Senchas and the great Book of Knowledge was called En Senchus Mor. This druidic class of storytellers told the mythology, history, genealogy, religious rituals, Brehon laws, herbs and medicine, and elements of the natural world. These professional storytellers were trained for years until every word was memorized.

Then they went out to teach and practice their craft. I have assigned the dates after reading and reasoning for my best guesses based on genetics, archeology, and changes in the climate. The following paragraphs summarize elements of the six invasions:

Fomorians.
Nine thousand years ago. Forever.

Whether peaceful arrivals or not, later invaders fought the giant sea pirates, the Fomorians, whose strongholds were the Tory Islands nine miles off County Donegal. They were said to have lived forever in the north. I wondered which genetic population they might have been. Were they possibly the earliest hunter-gatherers of a Y DNA that no longer exists? Were they early Norsemen? Or did they simply represent the forces of darkness for all who followed? Two distinct early stone tool types—microliths, and butt- and distally-trimmed blades dating to nine thousand years ago—were found in the north near Derry by archeologists.

1st Cesair.
Seven thousand five hundred years ago.

The first of six invasions traditionally listed is Cesair, a queen, and daughter of Noah, who escaped just ahead of the rising flood, landing in Bantry Bay in County Cork. To me, this may refer to Noah's flood, seven thousand five hundred years ago when the salt water of the Mediterranean broke through the Bosporus to raise the former freshwater lake, now the Black Sea, to current sea level. Or, if Cesair was sojourning in the Iberian refuge, it may have referred to the rising glacial meltwater of the Irish Sea between seventy-five hundred and six thousand years ago, before which the islands were part of the continent. Either way, it places her in Ireland in the same time frame. I imagine her to be clan mother, U4, Ursula, or H, Helena, genetically.

2nd Parthalon.
Seven thousand years ago.

The second invasion was of the Parthelonians who seem to me to match up with the early farmers. Geneticists identify the farming men as G2 and I2, and the women as H1, H3, U5, and V. But now the ancient DNA of G men in Ireland represent only one percent of the population today. These, having merged with existing hunter-gatherer populations, may have been the builders of the megaliths of Newgrange, Knowth, Dowth and Loughcrew.

Parthalon arrived from the east along the Mediterranean Sea landing near Donegal. The myth relates that Parthalon introduced agriculture, married Dealgnaid, had four sons, and divided Ireland in four parts. He established just laws regarding fostering children, cauldron making, and drinking ale. The Parthalonians established rules around hospitality. Archeological remains of domesticated ox were found on Dalkey Island off Dublin. They were thought to have sheep, goats, and cattle. They cleared forests for farming and pasturage. Indeed, eighteen thousand polished stone axes have been found in Ireland. Pollen records show they grew cereals. Excavations at Ceide Fields in County Mayo showed fields marked by court and or portal tombs. Some experts believe these marked family territories as deeds of ownership.

Legend tells that they flourished for a long time, reaching a population of nine thousand before they all died in the same week of May. Why did they die so suddenly? The plume from a volcanic eruption may cause darkness, but scientists would see evidence of ash in the geologic record as well, and I think even an extremely virulent plague would have taken more than a week to kill everyone. My best guess was that a meteorite struck close enough to have caused a form of winter. Scientists, by studying the growth rings of ancient trees, can see the season a meteorite may have struck Earth. Sunlight would be obliterated or dimmed causing all living things to suffer or die during the event of darkness. By counting and measuring the width of the tree rings, they then can see the length and severity of the event.

3rd Nemed.
Six thousand years ago.

Nemed, a son of Noah, left his Scythian home with his wife, Macha, and their four sons and wives. They arrived soon after the plague. The reference to the Scythians may link the Nemedians to an early wave of Corded Ware pottery people from the Pontic Steppe invaders. These were R1b1 men, also known as the Yamnaya, ancestors of the men who in the future would overwhelm the earlier male genetic lines. The DNA of the women most closely associated with these men were H, U5, T2, and T1 in order of diminishing percentages. To make these designations seem more like the real women they were, geneticist Bryan Sykes called them Helena, Ursula 5, Tara 2, and Tara 1.

They settled in Armagh, meaning Macha's hill, where they built a fortress, and in County Antrim where they built a second fortress. Their chief druid, Mide, for whom County Meath is named, lit the first ceremonial fire at Uisneach that blazed for seven years. This was the site, the center or naval of their world, from which the kings lit their own fires. That the Nemedians cleared fields in dense forests may relate to opening up pasturage for cattle and horses if they were the same herders of the Corded Ware pottery heritage from the Steppes.

After many battles, and losing the last one, they became the slaves of the Fomorians. Or they were made their vassals. These Nemedians may have been earlier R1B1 entrants to Ireland before their relatives arrived en masse in a later invasion. Myth says some escaped to Greece, some say to Belgium, to become the ancestors of the Fir Bolg, and some escaped to the North of Britain to become the Tuatha de Danaan. They will return.

4th Fir Bolg.
Five thousand years ago.

Myths claim the Fir Bolg arrived in Malahide Bay near Dublin during Lughnasa, the first of August, many generations after the Nemedians scattered. They had escaped slavery from Belgium or Greece where they labored hauling dirt in leather bags by turning the bags into boats. King Eochaid MacAirt and his wife Tailtiu established a peaceable kingdom dividing Ireland in four parts for their sons.

Myth compiler, Lady Gregory, said the Fir Bolg had no law but love, no religion, and that there was peace and plenty. Interestingly, there is no mention of Fomorians during the reign of the Fir Bolg. Had they forged an alliance or treaty?

Is it possible the Fir Bolg are related to the archeologically known Bell Beaker folk of Iberia and the Netherlands?

By four thousand years ago, many forests had been opened up for farming and pasturage to graze cows, horses, and wool-bearing sheep.

5th Tuatha de Danaan.
Four thousand five hundred years ago.

These are the tribes of the god of three skills. Tuatha means tribes; Danaan means of Anan. Arriving in a dark cloud before Beltine, the first of May, they settled on a mountain in the west. The dark cloud may relate to the catastrophic eruption of the volcano Hekla 4 four thousand years ago.

Descended from Nemedians who escaped north, they were healers, masters of the arts, of smithcraft, poetry, and song. A white cow was their goddess and the warrior, Lug, their god. They defeated the Fir Bolg and Fomorians in epic battles at Mag Tuired to win the right to rule Ireland at Tara. Three sons of Dagda divided Ireland and married three goddesses who excelled in a long list of arts and skills. They then built a great fort at Ailech in County Donegal at Inishowen Head. (This became the seat of the Ui Neill until it was seized in AD 425.)

The Tuatha de Danaan ruled for thousands of years until the arrival of the Milesians who defeated them. However, the Tuatha de Danaan was a magical race of ever-living beings. The Milesians and they divided the world in two, one above ground for the Milesians. The other world below was an idyllic, ageless place of beauty which the Tuatha de Danaan thereafter were forced to inhabit. The underground world was accessed through sidhs, or fairy mounds.

Celtic metalwork and design began in the trading Hallstatt Culture north and east of the Austrian Alps in the early Iron Age two thousand nine hundred years ago. The artistic style culminated in the breathtaking bronze, silver, and gold work of the La Tene-style people who flourished between two thousand five hundred to two thousand fifty years ago. Their intricate designs are considered the epitome of Celtic art. Were these cultures the origin of the Tuatha de Danaan? Are they also R1B1 Yamnaya descendants who contributed to the overwhelming R1B1 male gene pool of the British Isles and Ireland?

6TH MILESIANS.
Three thousand five hundred years ago.

It seems clear that everything changed dramatically after the arrival of the Milesians. These, then, were the final wave of people from the Steppes, the Bronze Age warriors of the Corded Ware pottery heritage. If the Tuatha de Danaan ruled for thousands of years, and the Milesians were the last invaders or arrivals, then I wondered if the Milesians may be Bell Beaker people of R1B1 who had settled in Spain. Not the earlier Fir Bolg from Belgium, but those from Iberia from four thousand five hundred years ago. Or the Milesians may have been a different group of people arriving in Ireland from the Basque Refuge in Spain, or Iberia.

Mil Espaine, a soldier of Spain, claimed origins from Noah, and Scythia as well. He was married to Scota, a noble Irishwoman, with whom they had sons. He died in Spain, but knew they were to go to Ireland from a druid, even though they had never seen it. A son built a high tower from which he glimpsed a shore of the land of the oracle. After reaching Ireland, he was treacherously killed on the way to his ship after meeting three kings of the Tuatha de Danaan at Ailech, in Derry.

The sons of Mil returned to conquer Ireland. They landed at Inber Scene to defeat the Tuatha de Danaan. After meeting three kings at Tara, they were tricked into leaving Ireland. A brewing storm threatened to wreck their ships, but they were saved by the recitation of a poem by the poet, Amergin, that stilled the waters. Once again on Irish soil his brother, Eremon, led the remaining brothers around Ireland in a sunwise turn to the Boyne River estuary to bring them luck. A sunwise turn is accomplished by keeping the object to the right of the person as he or she moves in a circle around the object, the well, the house, or the world.

Meeting the Tuatha de Danaan at Tailtiu (Teltown in County Meath) and Druim Ligen (near Rapoe, County Donegal) they were soon crushed. Once again, Ireland was divided among them with the widow of Mil, Scota, naming all the Irish people the Scoti. As a side note, a thousand years later a large group of Irish people, the Dalriada, migrated to nearby Alba from Ulster. The inhabitants in Alba referred to these newcomers as the Scoti, but after hundreds of years of warring, intermarrying, and settling in, all of Alba came to be called Scotland.

There is no hearth like your own hearth.

VII

Chief Irish Festivals and Gods

Festivals

Festivals are celebrated on the quarter year on the day in the middle cycle of the sun, between a solstice and an equinox. Bonfires are lit at hilltops and homes. Festivals begin on the eve.

- February 1: Imbolg, the goddess Brigid, daughter of Dagda and patron of poetry, crafts and healing. The Green Man is celebrated now.
- May 1: Bealtine, mouth (beal) or bright light (bel) plus tine, means fire and celebrates fertility, the open pasturing, and crops. Bonfires are lit.
- August 1: Lunasa, honoring the god Lugh who is young, beautiful, and athletic. All celebrate the bountiful harvest.
- November 1: Samain, when the tombs are opened to allow the spirits of the dead to emerge and mingle

with the living. People dress in costume to fool the spirits. It is All Hallow's Eve.

IMPORTANT IRISH GODS AND GODDESSES OF HISTORY

- Dagda. He is a good god who kills his enemies with one end of his club and heals them with the other end. His cauldron is always full of food.
- Morrigan. She is a goddess of war and tribal mother who protects her people in battle. She is a prophet and raven, the symbol of death.
- Lugh. Lugh is a god of arts, music, poetry, and storytelling. He is a harpist, sorcerer, champion in sports, and a craftsman. He protects the harvest and provides a good time.

Entrance at the six-thousand-year-old megalith at Knowth.

VIII

Ancient Irish Law

The Brehon were a scholarly class of people. They specialized in interdisciplinary lore as an elite group of poets, druids, and judges. Kings did not initiate laws, but were subject to them.

Every person had a value or honor price. If a crime was committed against that person, he or she was accordingly owed the price in goods or slaves. Poets had the highest honor price. If a person refused to grant hospitality or other serious offense, their honor price was reduced. All people had a social obligation to provide needed food and shelter for others. Even a king could not refuse those seeking help.

The Brehon determined one's value or honor price and the compensation to be paid in a legal dispute. For serious crimes, the next generation continued to pay the fine if necessary. However, if the perpetrator was proven ignorant of the law, the fine was cut in half. Unfair legal decisions could be redressed. Laws governed accidents and injuries.

To build bonds of community and loyalty, children were fostered out of their families to others. Boys returned home at seventeen, girls at fourteen, the ages of marriage.

While satire for poets was prized, there were laws against mocking someone's appearance or giving a person an offensive nickname.

Women might be trained as poets or warriors. A wife owned what she brought with her to the marriage. Household work done by either partner was given credit. Divorce was allowed. Slaves had rights. A pregnant slave was emancipated.

Ogham stones.

IX

Trees

Beyond the memories of any living Irish, history tells of the dense, deep forests that once covered much of Ireland. Indeed, trees, sacred groves, and the belief that all things were imbued with a god or spirit were integral to the druidic, pre-Christian Irish. The Irish alphabet, Ogham, is based on each letter represented by a tree and a portion of the year, with a special name and date for a tree of power, the Bile Buadha, on the 31st of October.

The Bile Buadha was planted in a sacred area outside the rath, or ringfort, of a king. Sacred groves planted at a church or holy site were considered a sanctuary and were protected by law.

In the ancient times the five most sacred trees of legend were:

- The Bile Tortan, an ash tree near Tara.
- The Craebh Daithi, an ash tree at Farbill in County Westmeath.

- The Craebh Uisnigh, also an ash at Uisniche, County Westmeath.
- Eo Mugna, an oak tree at Moone, County Kildare.
- Eo Rossa, a yew tree at Old Leighlin in County Carlow.

Laws existed to protect trees on an individual's property with fines for cutting or damaging the trees. The laws categorized trees in four classes: nobles of wood, commoners of wood, lower divisions of wood, and bushes of the wood. The noble class consisted of oak, hazel, holly, yew, ash, pine, and apple.

The Irish names for various trees are found in many place names of towns and locations throughout the land.

The Brian Boru oak.

THE OGHAM ALPHABET

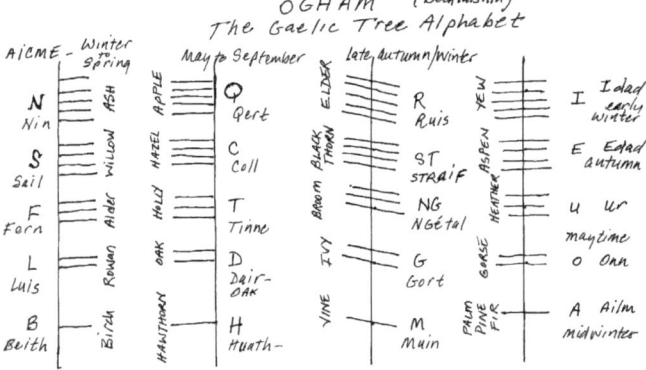

* Read from the bottom up, the way a tree is climbed. Names fall into three categories:
  1. Tree names — Beth, Fern, Sail, Dair, Coll, Onn, Edad and Idad.
  2. Poetic alternatives based on elements of the Trees, esp. when names have same first letter.
  3. Arboreal Themes.

* Please see *Irish Trees: Myths, Legends & Folklore*, by Niell Mac Coitir
  and *Ogham: The Celtic Oracle of The Trees*, by Paul Rhys Mountfort
  and *The Meaning of Trees: Botany, History, Healing, Lore*, Fred Hageneder

Appendix 1
Pronunciation of Modern Irish

Excerpted from James MacKillop's Oxford Dictionary of Celtic Mythology.

a	father
á	law
e	end
é	came
i	it
í	each
o	pull (Note from author: Old Irish was o as in o̱dd)
ó	ode
u	pull
ú	spoon
bh	before or after a or u: walrus
bh	before or after e or i: sliver
c	before or after consonants: climate
ch	before or after a or u: Bach or loch
ch	before or after e or i: hit
d	like dh
dh	before and after a and o: rogo (Spanish)
dh	before and after e or i: y (English)
fh:	silent

gh	before and after a and o: rogo
gh	before and after e or i: English y
mh	before and after a or o: walrus
mh	before and after e or i: sliver
s	before and after a or o: song
s	before and after e or i: ship
sh:	hope
T	before and after a or o: thought
t	before and after e or i: tune (British)
th:	hope

* * *

P-Celtic split from Q-Celtic approximately three thousand years ago. P-Celtic: Gaulish, Welsh, Cornish and Breton (Brythonic) as in the time of Caesar's Britain. Q-Celtic (goidelic): Irish, Scottish, Gaelic, Manx. For example: In Q-celtic Irish, the word for head is *caenn*. In Welsh, the word for head is *pen*.

Appendix 2
Irish Place Names

abh – river
achadh – field
ard or aird – hill, height or high place
ath – new
áth – ford
baile – farm, settlement (bal, bally)
bán – white
béal – estuary
bile – tree, meeting place
bóther – road
buidhe – yellow
bun – bottom
caiseal – ringfort
caisleán – castle (cashel)
caol – strait, narrow
carraig, carreg – rock, crag
cill – church or monastery
cloch, clochán – stone, rocky ruin
cluain – pasture
cnoc (knock) – rounded hill, mountain
corr – rounded hill
crois – cross
currach – bog, marsh
cong – isthmus
daingean – stronghold
dearg – red
díseart – hermitage
doire – grove, oakwood
domnach – an early church (donagh)
droichead – bridge
droim – ridge, mountain crest
dubh – black, dark
eanach – marsh
éar – east
eas – waterfall
fearn – alder tree

glas – grey, green, blue (or a mix)
gleann – glen
gort – field
inis, inish – island (inch) (innis)
íochtar – lower
lag – hollow
liag – stone
lios – fortified enclosure
loch, lough – lake
machaire – plain (magh)
mhór – big (mor) big
muillean – mill
nug – new
poll – cove, pool, hollow
ráth – circular fort
ribhach – grey or mottled
rinn – promontory
ruadh – red
sliabh – mountain (slieve)
slige, sligeach – shelly (sligo)
spidéal – hospital, place of hospitality (spital)
teampall – temple
tobar – spring, well
trá(igh) – beach, shore
tulach – hill
uisce, uisge – water

Appendix 3
Geneaology or Family Tree

Add your genealogy or family tree here.

Appendix 4

Travel List of Items to Pack for Ireland

Items to Pack:

- Passport
- Medications
- Money, foreign currency, credit cards
- Phone and charger, plus extra charger
- Computer, Kindle, iPad
- Earphones
- Books, puzzles, Sudoku
- Sunglasses, glasses
- Calendar and contacts, in print
- Itinerary
- Art supplies
- Gifts
- Pin number, travel numbers for airlines
- Fan
- Maps and GPS
- Instant coffee
- Earplugs
- Toothbrush and toiletries
- Sewing kit
- Ziploc bags, zip ties
- Solar, hand generator
- Water purification system
- Lightweight daypack
- Laundry soap
- Folding cup
- Copies of credit cards and passport in a secure location
- International or domestic carry-on-sized suitcase with four wheels
- Half-sized four-wheeled briefcase, or backpack as personal carry-on

TRAVEL ITEMS TO PACK *(continued)*

ESSENTIAL CLOTHING:

- Raincoat, long or 3/4 length
- Rain jacket with rain pants
- Featherweight anorak or wind jacket
- Evening shoes, evening dress
- Jewelry
- Slippers
- Lightweight, waterproof boots
- Water sandals
- Boots for town
- Walking shoes
- Bathing suit
- Pajamas
- Billed cap, knit cap, gloves,
- Midge net with lightweight, crushable brimmed hat
- Scarves, shawls
- Socks
- Pants
- Shirts

Appendix 5
Travel Tips for Packing for Ireland

Midge nets:

In Ireland and Scotland midges are not big floppy freshwater hatches of fish food, but clouds of tiny biting insects that love the carbon dioxide from your breath, and the moisture from your eyes and ears. If you're going out in the countryside and you don't know if it's midge season, stuff a midge net in your pocket to unroll over the brim of your hat just to be sure. Make sure the net has small enough holes to keep those tiny guys out. I've not experienced them in Ireland, but I take my net anyway.

Raincoats and waterproof boots:

Either take a real raincoat, at least two-thirds length, with a hood that has a drawstring and brim or buy one immediately when you arrive. If you plan to hike or visit the islands, take waterproof pants as well. I love sitting outside on a boat deck in the wind and rain knowing I'll be toasty warm and dry even if the interior seating is full. Boots for hiking or hill walking should be lightweight and waterproof. I always take a flyweight anorak folded into its pocket in my daypack or purse.

Gifts:

Ideal gifts are authentic items from home that are lightweight enough to pack. If not a poem, song, or dance to share, then I take scarves, Petoskey stones, aprons with cherries printed on them (my home is the

Travel Tips for Packing *(continued)*

cherry capital), dried cherries, and CDs of early jazz and blues artists. At one country house hotel, I left an apron to be given to the chef with apologies for its feminine design the night before we left. The next morning the breakfast room was atwitter. The server told me as I sat at our table that the chef loved the gift and wrote me a thank-you note. It was a paper folded on my plate. I flipped it open to discover a photo printed on it of the quite hairy chef wearing only the cherry covered apron without a stitch on underneath, arms spread wide in thanks and a huge smile. "I love the apron, sorry I'm not a lady chef." We all had a terrific laugh.

Medications:

Take your usual prescription meds with a copy of the prescription, as well as at least a few of any over-the-counter medications you might need under a variety of circumstances. Pack a decent first aid kit. Include moleskin and blister bandages. Liquid medicines may be taken away at customs, so try to take only dry medicine. Have available your prescriptions. I carry Polysporin and saline gel to keep my nostrils moist, and antibacterial lotion with me in all group settings, especially the airplane.

Clothes:

For women, take colorful silk scarves to jazz up the usual black, brown, or blue pants, skirts, and shirts. Silk packs incredibly lightly and can be washed in the sink and dried on a towel or hanger.

Jewelry:

Take fun, inexpensive pieces that you don't mind losing, and won't target you to thieves.

Documents and credit cards:

Keep copies where you can access them and others can't. Memorize pin numbers. Leave copies with someone at home.

Toiletries:

Among the usual, take a small bar of soap and a washcloth just in case you stay in the barest of accommodations. I take several small bottles of shampoos and lotions. As one is used I recycle it making room as I go. Take quart and gallon size Ziplock bags. Take your favorite clothes washing granules. In Europe, I wash most of my clothes by hand in the sink or tub, squeeze out the water, roll the clothes in a towel, stand on that to absorb the excess, then hang items out or drape them on the warming heaters.

Extras:

These items don't take much room, but might save the day: zip ties in several sizes (keep them in an outer pocket to secure your bag's zipper if needed), fish line, a small roll of duct tape, tiny flashlights that clip to the suitcase, a folding knife with scissors and wine opener (pack in checked luggage), extra cords for electronics, a solar or hand charger, Ziplock bags for everything from muddy boots to the day's lunch. I take Tyvek mailers to ship gifts or extra clothes home, and break the packing tape from the dispenser, step on it, and stuff it in the corner of my suitcase. Do not pack batteries in stowed luggage. Carry them on.

Packing Cubes:

Buy super lightweight, zippered nylon boxes of different colors for all of your clothes. Pants fit in one larger size, shirts have a special folding

Travel Tips for Packing *(continued)*

version, underwear, tank tops, scarves, and pajamas have their own cubes. When you open your suitcase, or if U.S. Customs officials do, you'll be happy to have everything neat and in its place. It's a snap to unpack and repack. Just place the cubes in the drawers or on shelves and you're done. I take a superlight zippered duffle bag or a featherweight daypack. When I arrive, all my outerwear goes into that and onto the back seat or trunk.

Suitcase:

Lighten up! A great, lightweight suitcase with four wheels that fully-packed weighs only twenty-five to thirty-five pounds is perfect for lifting into overhead bins and dragging up the stairs. Try for an international carry-on or the slightly larger domestic carry-on. Or buy a high quality backpack with wheels of the same size. For my personal carry-on I use a small four-wheeled bag or briefcase packed with one overnight's essentials, plus whatever I want on board, and all my valuables. I leave enough room for a smaller purse to go inside it.

Christy Barry, Michael Kelleher, Collin Nea, and Dave Lees at O'Connors Pub in Doolin.

Appendix 6
Irish Timeline

379-405	Niall of the Nine Hostages, king at Tara, father of the province of Ulster and the Ui Neill dynasty.
400-800	Dalriada, the kingdom of counties Antrim, Ireland and Argyll. Scotland thrives.
432	St. Patrick arrives in Ireland.
500	Europeans study at Irish monasteries.
554	Columba, the monk, establishes a monastery at Kells.
549	Yellow plague.
600	The end of the Old Ulliad, kingdom of East Ulster.
664	Yellow plague.
700	Armagh under Ui Neill control.
795	Viking raids on Scotland and Ireland.
841	Dublin founded by Vikings.
850	Irish kings fight Vikings and Danes for dominance.
902	Dublin Vikings defeated.
950	Vikings settle on River Lee in Cork.
1000	Brian Boru, becomes king of Munster, and half of Ireland.
1014	Brian Boru fights the Ostmen and English mercenaries. He dies.
1050	O'Connor, the last high king of Ireland.
1066	Battle of Hastings in England.
1100	A century of Anglo-Norman war, foreign invasion, and church reform.

IRISH TIMELINE *(continued)*

1101 — Synod of Cashel: taxes, celibacy, laws regarding marriage.
1102 — Priests forbidden to marry in England.
1127 — Cormac's chapel, Cashel begun.
1152 — Irish Church divided into four archbishoprics, Armagh (head), Dublin, Cashel, Tuam. New laws regarding marriage instituted.
1154 — Henry II becomes king of England.
1169 — Anglo-Norman mercenaries recruited by Diarmit MacMurchada, king of Leinster. Anglo-Norman invasion begins.
1170 — Strongbow, Richard Fitzgilbert de Clare, earl of Pembroke, captures Waterford and Dublin.
1171 — Irish kings and Normans submit to Henry II of England.
1172 — Christ Church Cathedral in Dublin founded.
1173 — King Henry II defeats baronial rebellion.
1177 — John de Courcy invades and occupies eastern Ulster. He builds ten forts, three castles, and six abbeys/monasteries.
1183 — Rory O'Connor, last king of Ireland, abdicates.
1185 — Prince John arrives in Waterford as lord of Ireland with Gerald de Barry. They take over the Suir Valley and antagonize the locals.
1205 — Hugh de Lacy takes over for de Courcy.
1208-1213 — England under papal interdict.
1216 — Prince Louis of France invades England.

1243	Ulster becomes a possession of England. Edward, son of Henry III, is appointed lord of Ireland.
1258	Baronial rebellion against Henry III.
1284	Stone walls built around Cork City.
1295	Irish army sent to support King Edward against the Scots.
1296	Scottish wars for independence.
1297	Englishmen forbidden to dress as Irishmen.
1298	Wallace defeats English at Falkirk in Scotland.
1300-1400	English colonizing of Ireland peaks this century.
1306	Robert the Bruce crowned king of Scotland.
1315	English defeat Edward Bruce's invasion of Ireland.
1327	Edward II deposed and murdered. Edward III.
1342	Edward III rules that all Irish, even of French or English descent, must be dismissed from all posts, and offices to be filled with English-born only.
1348-1350	Black Death.
1366	Statutes of Kilkenny are written forbidding Irish-Norman marriage.
1368	Absentee landlords ordered to return to defend their lands.
1371	Robert the II, first Stuart king of Scotland, Richard the II.
1387	Earls of Ormond and Desmond warring.
1394	Richard II comes to Ireland with thirty-four thousand troops until seventy-five Irish chiefs submit, but he is harassed in the mountains of Wicklow and flees without his army.

IRISH TIMELINE (continued)

1399	Henry IV becomes lord lieutenant of Ireland.
1446	Earls of Desmond and Ormond at war. Earls of Kildare rule.
1450	Richard Plantagenet, duke of York, becomes lieutenant of Ireland.
1453	War of Roses, Kildare and Desmond side with Lancaster, Ormond with York. Yorkists win the battle at Towton.
1483	Earl of Desmond becomes Irish, "gone native". The English murder Desmond's father in England and Desmond is implored to dress and act English. Earl of Kildare is the only powerful noble to support the crown.
1483-1485	Richard the III.
1485-1508	Henry the VII.
1494	Poyning's Law places Irish parliament under English authority.
1503	James IV of Scotland and Margaret Tudor marry.
1509-1533	Henry VIII. He marries Catharine of Aragon.
1541	Henry VIII made king of Ireland.
1556	Plantation of Kings (Laois) and Queens (Offaly) Counties.
1558-1603	Queen Elizabeth reigns.
1559	Protestantism restored. Mary Queen of Scots flees.
1569-1579	Fitzmaurice revolt, much fighting, the O'Neill and Desmond rebellions in Munster.
1570	Pope excommunicates Elizabeth.
1573	Attempted Plantation of Ulster.

1586	Plantation of Munster begins. English take one million acres for eighty-six families.
1587	Mary Queen of Scots is executed.
1588	Spanish Armada wrecked off Ireland.
1592	Trinity College established. Elizabeth I.
1595	Rebellion of Hugh O'Neill, Earl of Tyrone.
1601	English defeat Irish and Spanish forces at Kinsale.
1603	James VI king of England and Scotland.
1607	Flight of the earls to Europe, seeking aid against England ends Gaelic Ireland.
1609	Plantation of Ulster increases.
1613	Walls of Derry built.
1618	Forty-thousand Scots in Ulster. Irish moved to reservations.
1627	England at war with France.
1628	Oliver Cromwell enters parliament, which will not meet again until 1644.
1641	Rebellion in Ireland. Chaos. Ulster and Munster. Massacre of Protestants.
1641	Execution of Charles I.
1642	English Civil War.
1642	Confederation of Kilkenny, a Catholic assembly.
1649	Sieges of Drogheda and Wexford by Cromwell's forces. Much butchery. They kill one third of the Irish population. Roman Catholic worship is forbidden. Catholics flee or are sent to the West Indies.

Irish Timeline *(continued)*

1652	Act of Settlement pays English soldiers with Irish land.
1654	Cromwellian Plantation.
1658	Cromwell dies.
1662	Charles II marries Catharine of Braganza.
1673	Test Act excludes Catholics from office. Catholics are banished, schools are closed, eleven million acres are seized, Catholics sent west of the Shannon River to the poorest lands.
1678	Popish plot alleged in England created hysteria.
1688	Glorious revolution of William and Mary.
1688	Siege of Derry against the Catholic Earls of Antrim. Ten thousand people die.
1689	Siege of Derry for one hundred and five days. James II lands with Catholic (Jacobite) support. Fifteen thousand people starve behind the walls.
1690	Battle of the Boyne. Thirty thousand Catholics (the Jacobites) for James II fight against thirty-six thousand Protestants for William of Orange.
1691	Treaty of Limerick, defeat of Jacobites. "Wild Geese" exodus to Europe.
1695	Laws against Catholics and dissenters enacted.
1699	English laws against Irish woolen trade enacted.
1704	Test Act bars Catholics from holding office.
1707	England and Scotland joined in Act of Union.
1719	Castletown house in County Kildare begun.

1720	Westminster gains power to legislate for Ireland.
1726	Jonathon Swift publishes *Gulliver's Travels*.
1729	Parliament House in Dublin begun.
1731	Royal Dublin Society begun.
1745	Jacobite rebellion in England.
1756	Grand Canal construction begins from Dublin to Shannon and Barrow.
1760	George III.
1760	French land at Carrickfergus, Ireland.
1762	Britain declares war on Spain.
1765	Stamp Act passes taxing American colonies.
1775-1783	Revolutionary War in America.
1776	Troops sent to America from Ireland to fight in the Revolutionary War.
1778	Catholic Relief Act passed.
1780	Home Rule demanded in Ireland.
1782	Grattan's parliament establishes legislative independence.
1782-1881	Highland land clearances in Scotland.
1789	French Revolution.
1791	United Irishmen organization founded in Belfast to change laws.
1795	Orange Order founded in County Armagh.
1796	French Invasion fleet wrecked by weather in Bantry Bay.
1798	United Irishmen rebellion in Counties Wexford and Mayo brings stricter controls and much bitterness.

Irish Timeline *(continued)*

1799	Combination Act enacted to unite English and Irish parliaments, although Catholics must be a minority.
1800	Act of Union imposes direct rule from London for the next one hundred years. Ireland becomes part of Britain.
1811	George the Third's insanity.
1803	Robert Emmet rebellion in Dublin. *Emma*, by Jane Austen and *Ivanhoe*, by Walter Scott were written.
1823	Catholic Association established by Daniel O'Connell. National schools are established.
1828	Daniel O'Connell is elected Westminster MP (Member of Parliament).
1829	Catholic Emancipation Act. Catholics allowed seats in parliament.
1832	Cholera epidemic in England.
1840	Queen Victoria marries Prince Albert.
1845-1856	Potato blight. Great Famine begins, the worst year being in 1847. Many emigrate. Queen's Colleges established in Belfast, Cork, and Galway.
1848	Young Ireland's Rebellion rejects Daniel O'Connell's nonviolent politics.
1850	Irish Republican Brotherhood (IRB) funded by Irish Americans to bring about an Irish Republic.
1867	Fenian Rebellion attempts to gain Irish independence by force, bombings.
1871	Trade unions were established in England.
1873	Home Rule League founded.

1874	Ernest Shackleton born in Kilkeen.
1877	C.S. Parnell turns "Home Rulers" into a viable political party.
1880	Parnell leads Irish Parliamentary Party.
1882	Assassination of Lord Cavandish in Phoenix Park.
1884	GAA (Gaelic Athletic Association) founded.
1886	First Home Rule Bill is defeated.
1893	Gaelic League founded.
1897	*Dracula*, by Bram Stoker, and *The Gadfly*, by Ethel Voynich were written.
1890	Parnell ousted from Home Rule movement. Parnell scandal.
1903	Land Act established to allow tenants to purchase land with government aid.
1904	Abbey Theater opens.
1905	Sinn Féin founded: the Irish are free and no laws should be made without their consent.
1905	Ulster Unionist Council is formed. Irish Industrial Association is formed. Ancient Order of Hibernians is reorganized.
1909	Volta Theater in Dublin opens with James Joyce as manager.
1911	Titanic launched in Belfast.
1912	Titanic sank.
1913	Ulster Volunteer Force, Irish Volunteers, and Irish Citizens Army.

Irish Timeline *(continued)*

1913	Lockout strike in Dublin.
1914	England declares war on Germany.
1914	Home Rule bill passed, but not implemented. James Joyce's *Dubliners* published. Lusitania sinks off Cork coast.
1916	"Easter Rising" in Dublin, Irish Republic proclaimed. Sixteen leaders executed.
1919	First Dáil sits in Dublin following Westminster elections.
1919-1921	War of Independence for Ireland against England.
1919	IRA formed.
1920	Government of Ireland Act partitions Ireland.
1921	Truce. Anglo-Irish Agreement.
1922	Irish Free State established. They enact constitution.
1922	Michael Collins killed in ambush. *Ulysses* by James Joyce published in Paris.
1922-1923	Civil war in Irish Free State.
1923	W.B. Yeats receives Nobel Prize for Literature.
1926	George Bernard Shaw receives Nobel Prize for Literature.
1928	Women in England allowed the vote.
1932-1939	Economic war with Britain.
1937	New Constitution for Ireland/Eire.
1939-1945	England declares war on Germany. Ireland declares neutrality although ten thousand Irish serve with England.
1948	Irish Republic declared.
1949	Irish Republic is born.
1956-1962	Bombings and protest in Northern Ireland.

1964-1969	Civil rights protests lead to Northern Ireland Civil Rights Association.
1969	British troops arrive in Northern Ireland. Samuel Beckett receives the Nobel Prize in Literature.
1971	British Embassy burned in Dublin. Internment without trial in Northern Ireland.
1972	Bloody Sunday. Thirteen in Derry die. Stormont parliament is suspended. Direct rule from London.
1973	Republic of Ireland joins the European Economic Community, the EU. Sean MacBride, a founder of Amnesty International and human rights campaigner, wins Nobel Peace Prize.
1974	Ulster workers strike in Northern Ireland.
1976	British Ambassador assassinated in Dublin.
1977	Mairead Corrigan and Betty Williams receive Nobel Peace Prize.
1979	Earl Mountbattan assassinated in Sligo.
1981	Republican hunger strike in Northern Ireland, ten die, including MP, Bobby Sands.
1985	Anglo-Irish Agreement between governments.
1987	Remembrance Day bombing in Enniskillen. Eleven die.
1991	Mary Robinson becomes first female president of the Republic.
1993	Downing Street Declaration: Right of people of Ireland to self-rule and solve issues between the Republic and Northern Ireland by majority.

Irish Timeline *(continued)*

1994	Irish Republican Army (IRA) and Combined Loyalist Military Command agree on ceasefire.
1996	Seamus Heaney awarded Nobel Prize in Literature. IRA ceasefire ends. Canary Wharf bombing by the IRA.
1997	Resume ceasefire.
1998	Belfast Good Friday Agreement for Peace. David Trimble and John Hume awarded Nobel Peace Prize.
1999	Northern Ireland Assembly operating as regional parliament. National Museum opens in Dublin.
2000	Millennium Forest project to plant a tree for each member of the Republic was formed.
2002	Republic of Ireland currency becomes Euro. Northern Ireland Assembly suspended by Britain.
2003	Democratic Unionist Party (DUP) and Sinn Féin are the dominant political parties.
2004	Northern Ireland Assembly remains suspended.
2005	The IRA agrees to disarm voluntarily.
2006	Twenty year strategy launched to create bilingual Irish-English society.
2008	Global financial crisis sinks economy.
2010	Austerity program, EU bailout.
2013	Recession, Republic exits bailout program having fulfilled conditions.
2013	Taoiseach Enda Kenny formally apologizes for women detained and forced to work in the Magdalene laundries without pay between 1922 and 1966.

2013	Legislation passed allowing abortion in limited circumstances.
2013	Poet Seamus Heaney dies.
2014	Tax loophole closed allowing foreign multinationals to pay very low taxes.
2015	Referendum approves same-sex marriage by a large margin.
2016	Enda Kenny elected Taoiseach forming a minority government.
2017	Leo Varadkar elected prime minister after Enda Kenny resigns.

Entrance at six-thousand-year-old Newgrange.

Appendix 7: Prehistoric Timeline

	60-40 kya	40-20 kya	20-15 kya	15,000-10,000 ya
Notes / Myth	700,000-200,000 ya super-archaic humans — "Ghost" DNA	Prehistoric humans relate distance to the time it takes to get there. Hunter-gatherers expanded into new territory at the rate of 2-3 kilometers/year.	(1st) 14,000 ya Cesair arrives in Ireland	
DNA	Neanderthals and non-Africans interbreed. 50-40 kya. Denisovians interbreed with non-African San. Move East.	Hunter Gatherers from East to Western Europe. (WHG) 39 kya Neanderthals are extinct. Early people blend in the Franco-Cantabrian refuge — Basque. R1B1 YDNA + mtDNA U⁵, N, H (Helena) (Ursula) to Europe in Europe 25,000 ya. YDNA-IJ to G2, C1	I2 YDNA and U5 in Europe R1B9, R1B14. 15 kya Hunter-gatherer genes from SE and East blend with European H-Gs. mtDNA H3 arises from within Europe, possibly Sardinia. mtDNA H in Western Europe.	
Culture	A group of San people leave Africa. Begin to populate the non-African world. 60 kya. 40 kya Aurignacian Culture.	35 kya - 22 kya Gravettian Culture. Chauvet Cave paintings, in SW France. female Worship, Sewing needles used. 26 kya - Solutrean Culture	Magdalenian Culture	16-13 kya Older Dryas period of very cold climate send Northern people into refugia. 15 kya - Only Ice in Britain. 14 kya - Sudden warming → floods 11 kya - Britain repopulates, as does N. Europe. People and game flow east to west. FARMING BEGINS IN NEAR EAST
Nature / Climate	UPPER PALEOLITHIC ERA/AGE TO 10,000 ya	39 kya Campi Flegri Naples erupts. Ash over Pontic Steppe. Maximum Ice pushes South	LGM Last Glacial Maximum. Western Europeans move South to the Franco-Cantabrian Refuge (Basq)	In Ireland, grassland, deer, H-G, fishing. FLOOD ↓ Very cold ↓ 16 kya - 13 kya Older Dryas "Younger Dryas" 13 kya - 12 kya quick freeze 14,000 ya — Sudden warmth — Flood Alpine Ice melts
		← Last Glacial Maximum 25-15 kya →		
	← UPPER PALEOLITHIC AGE 50-10 kya →			WARMING

L. LEE

Notes / Myth

9000 ya: Irish myth of Fomorians—the giants from the North future invaders battled.

7500 YA or 14,000 YA
Ireland
1st invasion: CESAIR
2nd Invasion:
7500 YA - 6500 YA
Parthalon:
early farmers

DNA

West Eurasian populations blend. American Indians retain 1/3 of this ancestry as they migrate East.

YDNA G2a, mtDNA X2 arrived with early farmers.

YDNA- R1B1 in Franco-Cantabrian refuge, and migrating as H-G to England and Ireland when ice allows.

Evidence of first people in Ireland. Hunter gatherers.

West Eurasian populations collapse into each other blending DNA.

MTDNA HELENA (H) to Ireland

YDNA G2a
I, I2

Black Sea (from Ukraine)
On the Pontic Steppes, Anatolian Farmers + Hunter gatherers = **Corded wall pottery** people of Pontic Steppes developing wheeled carts, cattle herding, domesticating horses = Yamnaya.

First Farmers from Mediterranean route to Sardinia, Ireland.

Danube
Linear band Ceramic
7500-6500 ya
Seafaring.
Sheep in Italy
7000 ya:
Linen weaving,
Copper and gold ornaments.
Flint and obsidian tools.

Nature

HOLOCENE EPOCH "COMPLETELY NEW"

Mammoth habitat of grasslands are replaced by woodlands in Ireland.

FLOODING

Last glacier.
Black Sea Flood.
HEKLA Icelandic ERUPTS IN 7600 YA
Hazel, pine, Elm, Oak to Ireland. FLOOD

Ice between Ireland & Britain

MESOLITHIC ERA

10 - 9000 YA	9000 - 8000 YA	8000 - 7000 YA	6500

see Reich, David; Sykes, Bryan; Oppenheimer, Steven

Thank you, L. Lee

PREHISTORIC TIMELINE *(continued)*

Notes / Myths

- 5200 ya. Common language → GAULISH, GOIDELIC-Q Celtic, BRYTHONIC — **6th Invasion: Milesians** 4500 ← 3500 ya or earlier?
- **3rd Invasion: Nemed** 7500 ya to 7000 ya ← or earlier?
- **4th Invasion: Fir Bolg** 7000 ya ← or earlier? 6370 ya.
- **4th Invasion: Fir Bolg** 7000 ya – 6370 ya
- **5th Invasion: Tuatha de Danaan** 6370 to 4500 ya → or earlier?

Atlantic Megalithic Culture — 5500 — 6370 — 4500 — RM M269 SL23

DNA

- Hunter Gatherers + early farmers + Funnel Beaker people. YDNA I-1
- IRISH DNA 6500 ya
- YDNA G2a, I2a, J1, T. mtDNA: H1, H3, U4, U5b1
- 18,000 stone axes found in Ireland. "Passage from K to S" 3rd
- Abrupt change. Yamnaya, Corded Ware + Bell Beaker cultures from Pontic Steppes (R1B1) arrive in Ireland & Britain by coast. YDNA = R1B1
- Before, no Steppes DNA in Ireland. mtDNA arrive H5, R1a, NNa, T2, X2
- After, mostly Steppes + YDNA + Bell Beaker R1B1 in Ireland. R1B1: 90%. 1st farmers = 10%

Culture

- Cremation
- Ritual communal burial
- 1st portal tombs
- Wool-bearing sheep
- Late Mesolithic
- Court tombs, textiles
- Megaliths — Newgrange, Dowth, Knowth, et al. built in female, communal, place-based culture. FARMING 6000 – 4000 ya Neolithic Era
- Funnel Beaker
- Bell Beaker
- Abrupt change to mobile, horse riding, seafaring warriors, male dominated, alcohol, individualistic elites society. Metal trade, battle axes, carts, cattle herding, cavalry, chariots, archery, raiders. Flat graves for elite & men.

Nature

- Céide Fields in Co. Mayo, 6000 ya, early farmer dwellings on thousands of acres.
- Mammoth habitat of grasslands replaced by woodlands.
- Late Mesolithic Era
- 3rd Flood ✱ Water between Britain and Ireland
- 6370 Event: limit growth for Bog Oaks
- Clear fields of trees for farming. Permanent farming in Sardinia, 6000 ya. Obsidian in Sardinia. Single pot meals and drinking jars. Copper Age. plows
- COMETS
- Neolithic Age
- ASTEROIDS OF TAURIDS
- Urnfield burials. Burials with grave goods. Forest to pasture for herds. 4200 ya Hekla 4 erupts. 4807 Comet
- Ocean impact Asteroid • BRONZE AGE TO 3200 YA.

7000 – 6000 YA	6000 – 5000 YA	5000 – 4000 YA

7000 See Cunliffe, Barry Oxford   6000 – Illustrated History of Prehistoric Europe   5/80 Thank you, L. Lee

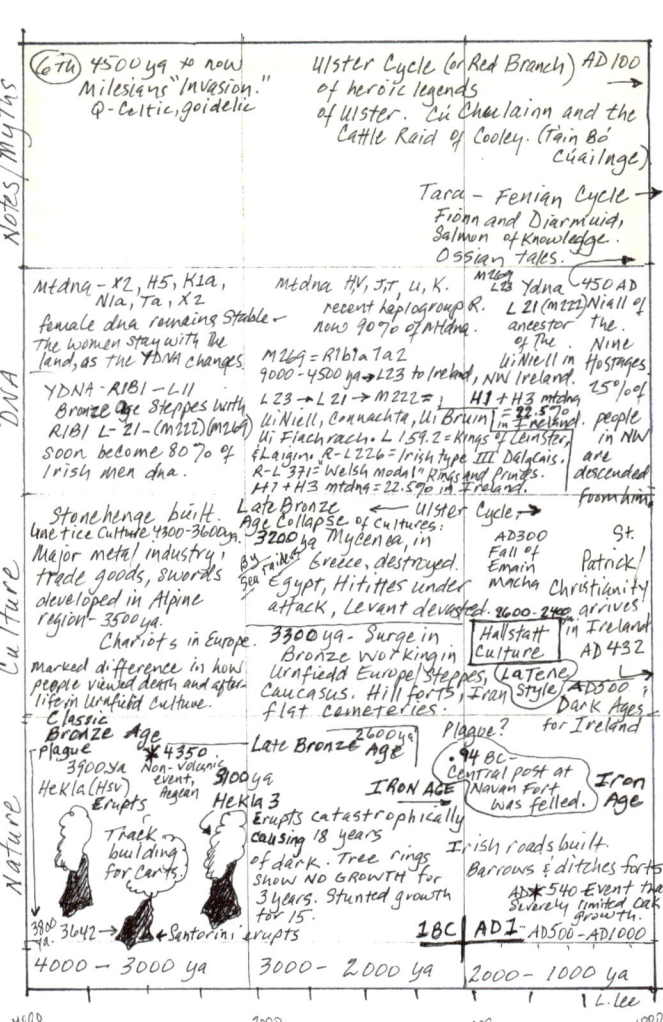

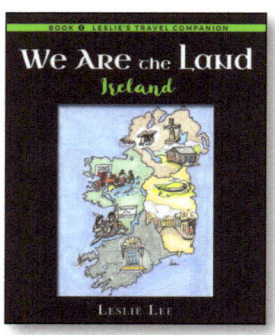

For the Reading List and Bibliography,
please refer to
We Are the Land: Ireland
by Leslie Lee
It may be ordered from your local bookstore, or at
LeeStudioTC.com.

Copies of maps and illustrations are available
as well through LeeStudioTC.com
or email: Info@LeeStudioTC.com

www.ingramcontent.com/pod-product-compliance
Lightning Source LLC
Chambersburg PA
CBHW041508010526
44118CB00006B/185